A KID'S GUIDE TO FEELING

FEELING LONELY

BY KIRSTY HOLMES

BookLife
PUBLISHING

©2018
BookLife Publishing
King's Lynn
Norfolk PE30 4LS

All facts, statistics, web addresses and URLs in this book were verified as valid and accurate at time of writing. No responsibility for any changes to external websites or references can be accepted by either the author or publisher.

All rights reserved.
Printed in Malaysia.

A catalogue record for this book is available from the British Library.

ISBN: 978-1-78637-270-3

Written by:
Kirsty Holmes

Edited by:
Holly Duhig

Designed by:
Danielle Rippengill

Image Credits

All images are courtesy of Shutterstock.com, unless otherwise specified. With thanks to Getty Images, Thinkstock Photo and iStockphoto. Front Cover – MarinaMay, yayasya, jirawat phueksriphan, Piotr Urakau, esthermm, mielag, AlenD, ViChizh, Voyagerix. Images used on every page – MarinaMay, yayasya, Piotr Urakau. 5 – johavel, Titov Nikolai, Makc. 5&6 – Rvector. 8 – kitisak pingkasarn, maxim ibragimov, narikan, esthermm. 9 – ViChizh, Eakachai Leesin, fasphotographic. 11 – AlenD, Voyagerix, Studio_G. 12 – mielag, Jenov Jenovallen, Gelpi. 13 – Tomacco, GoodStudio, vladwel. 14 – tupomi, Melody A. 15 – Monkey Business Images, VaLiza, aradaphotography. 16 – Poznyakov. 17 – LightField Studios. 18 – anna.danilkova. 21 – Life and Times, VaLiza, Flashon Studio. 21–23 – johavel, Titov Nikolai, Makc.

This book is to be returned on or before
the last date stamped below.

Schools

CONTENTS

Page 4   Introducing… Agents of F.E.E.L.S!

Page 8   How Do We Feel When We're Lonely?

Page 10   How Do We Look When We're Lonely?

Page 12   Why Do We Feel Lonely?

Page 14   Things That Make Us Lonely

Page 16   When Feeling Lonely Is Good

Page 18   When Feeling Lonely Is Bad

Page 20   Dealing with Feelings

Page 22   Let's Help!

Page 24   Glossary and Index

Words that look like **this** can be found in the glossary on page 24.

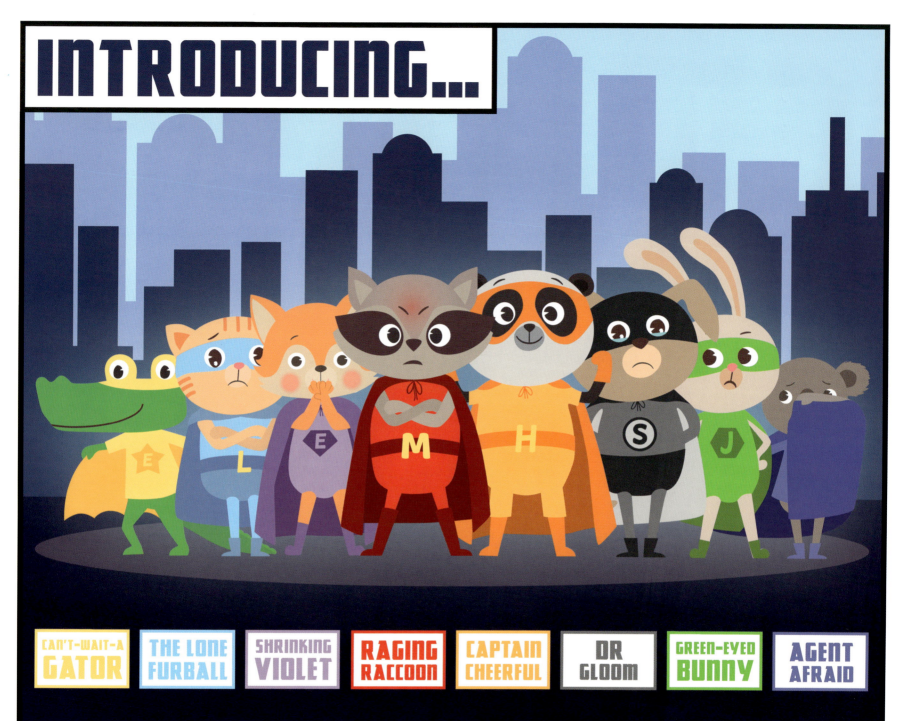

We all have **emotions**, or feelings, all the time. Our feelings are very important. They help us think about the world around us, and know how we want to **react**.

Sometimes, we feel good. Other times, we feel bad.

Everyone else is playing with a friend. Our hero is feeling pretty lonely.

Let's find out more… 7

HOW DO WE FEEL WHEN WE'RE LONELY?

You might feel an **ache** in your heart…

…you might feel **afraid** to speak…

…you might feel like you are empty inside…

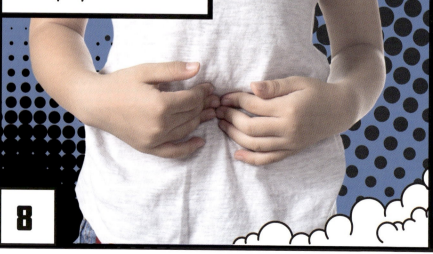

…or feel sad and want to cry.

8

HOW DO WE LOOK WHEN WE'RE LONELY?

WHY DO WE FEEL LONELY?

FEELING LONELY IS AN IMPORTANT EMOTION.

Thousands of years ago, humans lived on **plains**.

Some animals **hunted** people...

SAFETY IN NUMBERS!

FIND FRIENDS!

...so they stayed together for safety.

THINGS THAT MAKE US LONELY

MISSING OUR FRIENDS

MOVING TO A NEW AREA

FEELING SHY

14

You might feel lonely if you are new in a group…

…or if you fall out with your friends.

OH NO!

We can feel lonely if we are on our own, or even when we are not.

WHEN FEELING LONELY IS GOOD

Feeling lonely can help us. We might feel that we want to meet someone new, or make a new friend.

When we feel lonely, our minds are telling us that we need to be around people!

If we have been with people too long, we might feel tired. It's fine to want to be alone sometimes too.

WHEN FEELING LONELY IS BAD

Feeling lonely can make you feel sad and can make you feel left out.

It's OK to want to be alone sometimes, but our feelings of loneliness tell us when we need to be around people too.

It's not nice to feel lonely all the time.

DEALING WITH FEELINGS

Her friends will help her to feel better. Agents of F.E.E.L.S: GO!

If you want to play…

…try smiling first.

Maybe a grown-up could go with you?

Take a deep breath if you feel shy…

…and ask if you can play too.

21

LET'S HELP!

Talking about your feelings can help you to understand why you feel lonely.

GLOSSARY

ACHE	hurt with a dull, constant pain
AFRAID	feeling of fear or being scared
AREA	a place, region or location
ATTACK	cause harm, damage or hurt
BODY LANGUAGE	things a person does with their body that tell you how they feel
EMOTIONS	a strong feeling such as joy, hatred, sorrow, or fear
HUNTED	chased and killed for food or sport
PLAINS	large areas of flat land with a few trees
REACT	act or respond to something that has happened or been done

INDEX

ALONE 17, 19

ATTACK 13

CRYING 8

DEEP BREATHS 21, 23

FEELING BAD 5, 18

FEELING GOOD 5, 16

FRIENDS 7, 12, 14–16, 18, 20

GROUPS 13, 15

HEART 8

LEFT OUT 18

PLAYING 6–7, 9, 11, 21–23

SHYNESS 14, 21